# Introduction

I'm just an ordinary guy with a day job and a little bit of hope can grow into something...sometimes.

Just a short time ago, I saw a need for coloring books, activity books, and other products that were not aimed at children, and not so complex that older generations, and even stroke patients can use to keep their minds active, engaged, and entertained.

I decided to act quickly, created three coloring books as a start to fill the gap, and I'm creating more titles!! I welcome your feedback and hope to respond with more books that will help you and your loved ones stay active, engaged...and spry.

Here's to the art of staying young!

# Heartfelt Thanks

I'd like to thank Jon Acuff and his merry band of Dreamers, Builders, and Hustlers. Jon created an awesome community of people that helps you believe that dreams can come true. There are so many people there that I call friends, and have helped me, challenged me, and provided me with a valuable compass to help guide the way.

Do you have a dream? Let nothing stop you!

Help others find this product by reviewing it on Amazon!

We greatly appreciate your honest reviews.

**!** Post your artwork on social media to help spread the word and win prizes, use the hashtag #sprymind

We want to see your creation!

This, and other titles available on Amazon now:
Cars, Planes and More
Fabric Designer

Coming soon:
Color Me Peaceful
Patterns from Nature
A Colorful Journey

Find us:
Facebook: facebook.com/sprymind
Instagram: @mysprymind
Twitter: @mysprymind
Web: sprymind.com

Your purchase provides nursing homes, clinics and stroke patients with free copies of coloring and activity books.

This page intentionally left blank to protect your artwork

# Dream Big.

This design fits a standard 8 x 10 inch frame

This page intentionally left blank to protect your artwork

This design fits a standard 8 x 10 inch frame

This page intentionally left blank to protect your artwork

"I used to think God guided us by opening and closing doors, but now I know sometimes God wants us to kick some doors down."

Bob Goff

This page intentionally left blank to protect your artwork

This design fits a standard 8 x 10 inch frame

This page intentionally left blank to protect your artwork

This design fits a standard 8 x 10 inch frame

This page intentionally left blank to protect your artwork

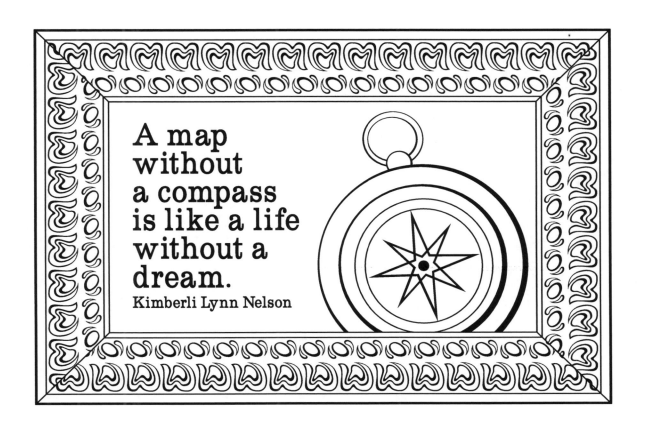

A map without a compass is like a life without a dream.
Kimberli Lynn Nelson

We are the captains of our destiny and our dream is the lighthouse guiding our voyage.
Chris Holmes

These designs fit a standard 4 x 6 inch frame

This page intentionally left blank to protect your artwork

# The best time to start...is NOW!

This design fits a standard 8 x 10 inch frame

This page intentionally left blank to protect your artwork

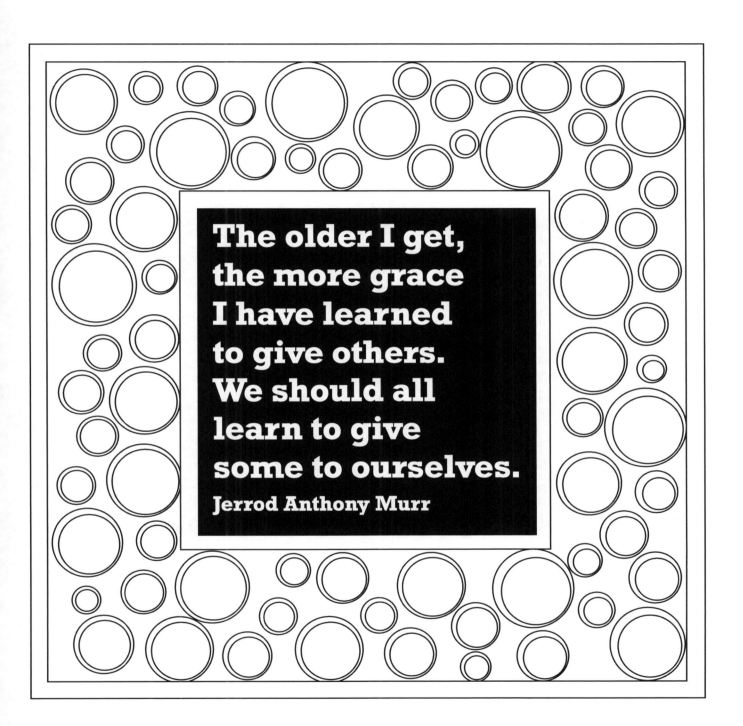

The older I get,
the more grace
I have learned
to give others.
We should all
learn to give
some to ourselves.
Jerrod Anthony Murr

This design fits a standard 7 x 7 inch frame

This page intentionally left blank to protect your artwork

Hope
is the
original
fear puncher
Jane Tuttle

This design fits a standard 8 x 10 inch frame

This page intentionally left blank to protect your artwork

This design fits a standard 8 x 10 inch frame

This page intentionally left blank to protect your artwork

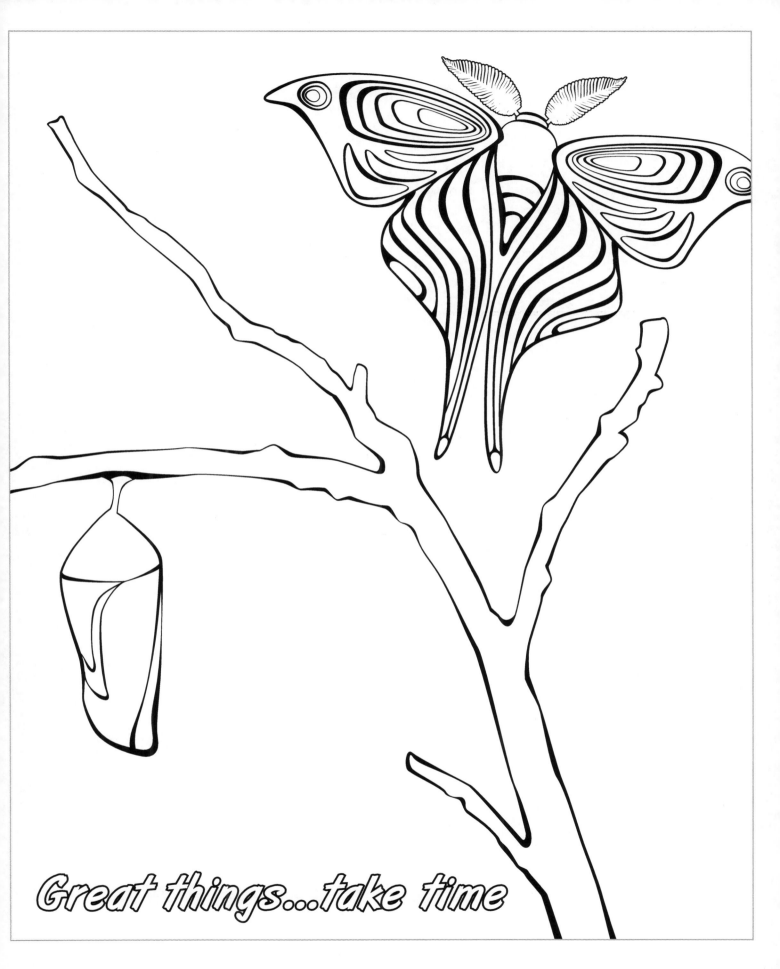

Great things...take time

This design fits a standard 8 x 10 inch frame

This page intentionally left blank to protect your artwork

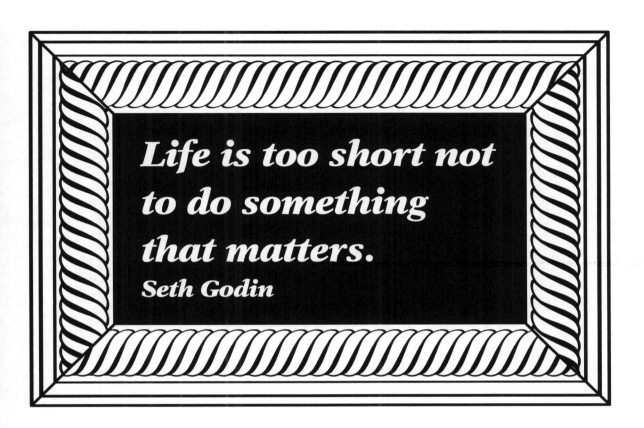

Life is too short not to do something that matters.
Seth Godin

bravery is a choice not a feeling [JON ACUFF]

Hand lettering by Rachel Mayo

These designs fit a standard 4 x 6 inch frame

This page intentionally left blank to protect your artwork

This design fits a standard 8 x 10 inch frame

This page intentionally left blank to protect your artwork

This page intentionally left blank to protect your artwork

Opportunity is missed by most people because it is dressed in overalls and looks like work.

Thomas Edison

This design fits a standard 8 x 10 inch frame

This page intentionally left blank to protect your artwork

Today is the perfect day to spread your wings and soar!

Amy Latta

This design fits a standard 8 x 10 inch frame

This page intentionally left blank to protect your artwork

# You don't have to go fast, you just have to GO!

This design fits a standard 8 x 10 inch frame

This page intentionally left blank to protect your artwork

This page intentionally left blank to protect your artwork

This page intentionally left blank to protect your artwork

Grace means we can quit sorting through our failures like we're trying to match socks.

Bob Goff

This design fits a standard 8 x 10 inch frame

This page intentionally left blank to protect your artwork

# SOMETIMES YOU FIND MOTIVATION... SOMETIMES MOTIVATION FINDS YOU

This design fits a standard 8 x 10 inch frame

This page intentionally left blank to protect your artwork

Some people develop a wishbone where their backbone should be.

This design fits a standard 8 x 10 inch frame

This page intentionally left blank to protect your artwork

have HOPE
BE strong LAUGH LOUD
live in the moment & PLAY HARD
smile often DREAM
REMEMBER you are BIG
loved AND NEVER give UP.
ever

This page intentionally left blank to protect your artwork

This design fits a standard 8 x 10 inch frame

This page intentionally left blank to protect your artwork

Your Future

Your past
doesn't define you.
April Best

This design fits a standard 8 x 10 inch frame

This page intentionally left blank to protect your artwork

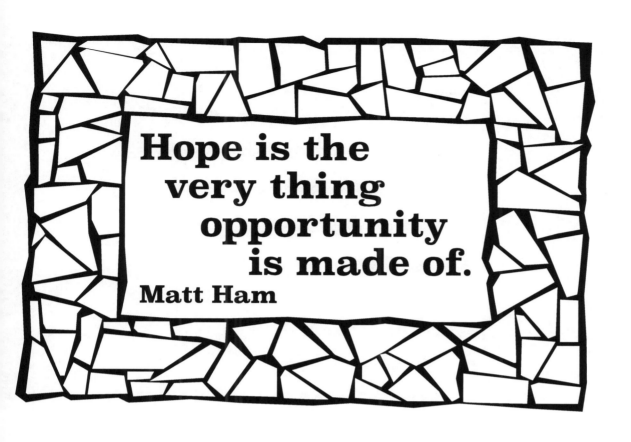

**Hope is the very thing opportunity is made of.**
Matt Ham

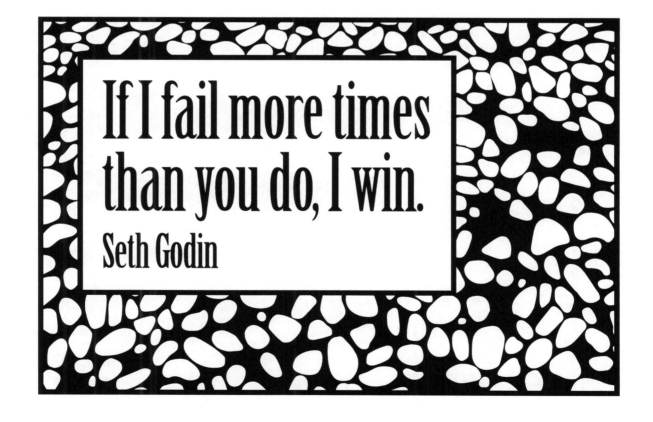

**If I fail more times than you do, I win.**
Seth Godin

This page intentionally left blank to protect your artwork

HOPE
FINDS
A WAY

This design fits a standard 8 x 10 inch frame

This page intentionally left blank to protect your artwork

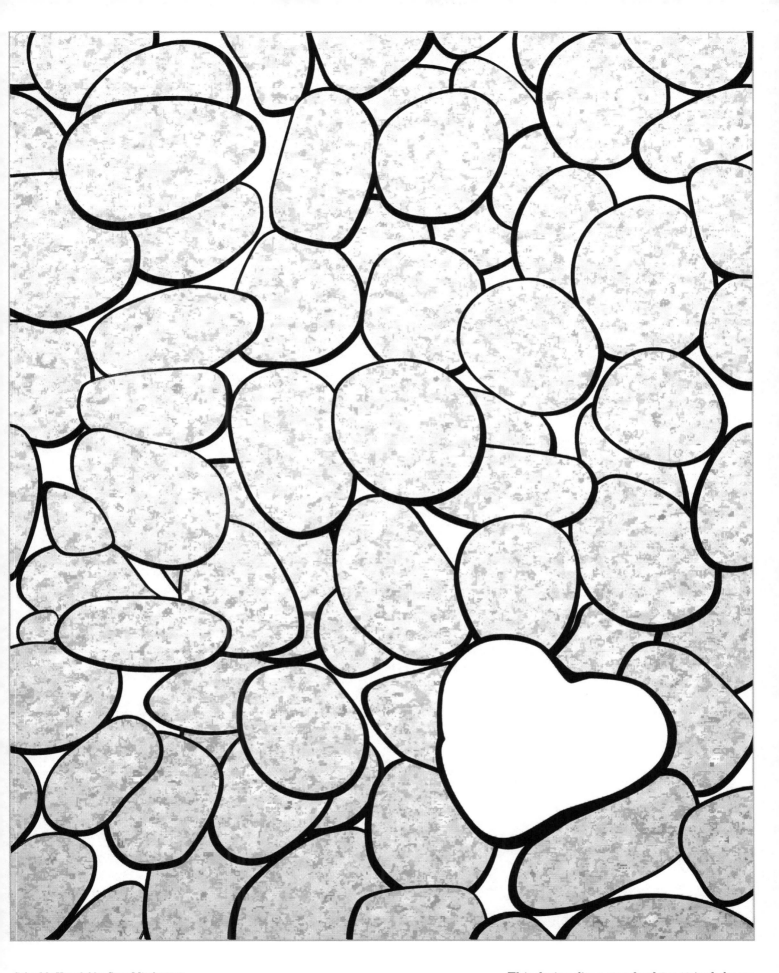

This design fits a standard 8 x 10 inch frame

This page intentionally left blank to protect your artwork

This page intentionally left blank to protect your artwork

Sometimes even Hope
needs a running start.
Laura Gutknecht

Life is too short
not to do something
that matters.
Seth Godin

These designs fit a standard 4 x 6 inch frame

This page intentionally left blank to protect your artwork

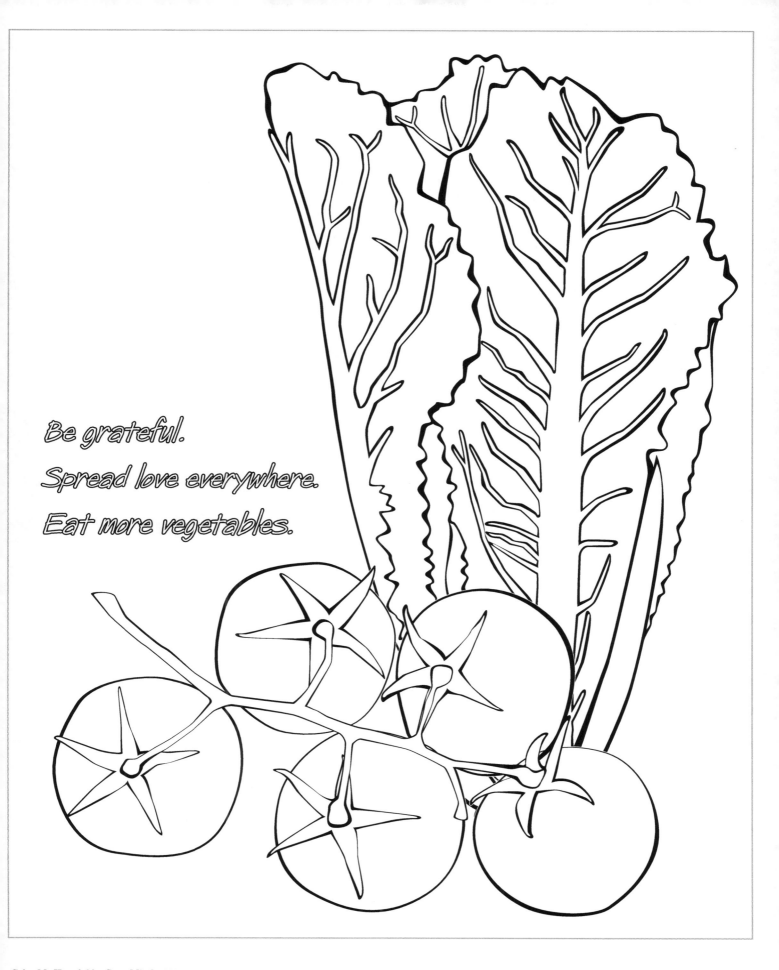

Be grateful.
Spread love everywhere.
Eat more vegetables.

This design fits a standard 8 x 10 inch frame

This page intentionally left blank to protect your artwork

# With Gratitude

I would like to express tremendous gratitude and thanks to those who contributed to this project:

Amy Latta (amylatta.com)

April Best (carelessinthecareofgod.com)

Bob Goff (bobgoff.com)

Chris Holmes (writerchrisholmes.com)

Dreamers and Builders (and there are so many of you!)

Jane Tuttle (twitter.com/janeatuttle)

Jerrod Anthony Murr (jerrodmurr.com)

Jon Acuff (acuff.me)

Kimberli Lynn Nelson (facebook.com/TransparencyBreedsFreedom)

Laura Gutknect (twitter.com/lauragutknecht)

Matt Ham (mattham.com)

Rachel Mayo (etsy.com/shop/RachelBDesigns)

Seth Godin (sethgodin.com)

Thomas Edison

Made in the USA
Middletown, DE
28 April 2016